IMAGES
of England

AROUND GILLINGHAM

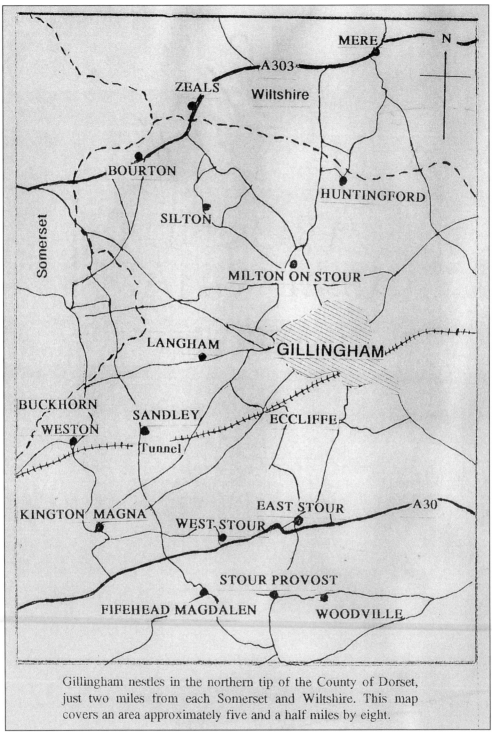

Gillingham nestles in the northern tip of the County of Dorset, just two miles from each Somerset and Wiltshire. This map covers an area approximately five and a half miles by eight.

Gillingham nestles in the northern tip of the county of Dorset, just two miles from both Somerset and Wiltshire. This map covers an area of approximately five and a half miles by eight.

IMAGES
of England

AROUND GILLINGHAM

Compiled by
David Lloyd

TEMPUS

Tempus Publishing Limited
The Mill, Brimscombe Port,
Stroud, Gloucestershire, GL5 2QG

ISBN 0 7524 1158 6

Typesetting and origination by
Tempus Publishing Limited
Printed in Great Britain by
Midway Clark Printing, Wiltshire

Also available in this series from Tempus Publishing:

Around Bridport
Around Bridport: the Second Selection
Christchurch
Dorchester
Glastonbury
Poole
Salisbury
Salisbury Plain
Salisbury Plain: the Second Selection
Shaftesbury
Sherborne and Milborne Port
Trowbridge
Around Uplyme and Lyme Regis
Yeovil

Contents

Acknowledgements

My special thanks go to Peter Crocker, chairman of the Local History Society, and Lyn Light, the honorary curator of Gillingham Museum, who have helped and encouraged me to complete this project, as well as my wife, Kathy, and sons, Andrew and Richard, for their endurance, assistance and understanding throughout the collection and preparation stages. Special thanks must also go to my father, Cliff, and late mother, Ivy, who helped so much with the identification of so many people in the group photographs.

I am also grateful to the following people and organisations that have loaned photographs, helped put names to faces and supplied other information:

Betty Allard, Tony Allard, Dick Arnold, Philip Arnold, David Ayles, Nick Baker, Nigel Bennett (Lloyds Bank), Mervyn Biss, Carola Bland, Mr and Mrs Sam Braddick, Bill Budden, Maj. Gen. Carrick, Bob Carter, Hilda Collier, Bruce Cook, Malcolm Cross, Mrs C. Cox, Ted Cull, Michael Dacre, Peter Daniels, Elaine Davis, Anita and Raymond Dear, Mr V. Duffett, Mr and Mrs Elsworth, Mr and Mrs E. England, Bertha Francis, Mr and Mrs R. Gallbally, Mr Gatehouse, Gillingham Museum, Gillingham School, Mrs P. Grace, Mrs D. Gray, Herbert Green, Owen Green, Les Gurnett, Mrs K. Harris, Mrs P. Hicks, John Hillier, Sonia Hillier, Di and Ken Hiscock, Robert Hooper, Don Hoskins, Alan Hoy, G. Herbert Hoy, Marion Hughes, Ivy Hull, Joan Jaggard, Beryl Knapton, John Knapton, Herbie Light, Mike Lloyd, Sue Lodge, Gordon Luffman, Jean Male, Jesse Martin, NatWest Bank, Roy Ozzard, Peter Mera, Jeffery Pink, Jess Pitman, Vic Pitman, Richard Phillips, Mr and Mrs Eric Proudley, Mrs V. Raymond, Phil Read, Mrs V. Richards, Rosie Roberts, Janet and Philip Robson, Michael Rose, Pat Rugman, Robert Smith, Mr and Mrs R. Stacey, Rex Standerwick, Ken Suter, Tommy Suttle, Mrs L. Taylor, Mr and Mrs Ken Taylor, Bill Trim, Phil and Peggy Wiseman, Sam Woodcock.

Thanks also go to those of you whom I have omitted to mention. Copies of photographs unused on this occasion will be saved for a future project and/or passed on to the Gillingham Museum.

Please send any correspondence relating to any of the photographs to me, c/o Gillingham Museum, Chantry Fields, Gillingham, Dorset SP8 4UA, or e-mail at Davidlloyd @ btinternet.com.

David Lloyd, 1998

Introduction

In 1992, I helped Peter Crocker, the chairman of the Local History Society, with his book of Gillingham photographs and I commented that there was plenty of unused material – 'You can do the next book', he said. So here it is – a collection of nostalgic photographs, mostly taken from my own personal collection, supplemented with images from Gillingham Museum and private archives.

To compile such a book has been a long-held ambition of mine, initiated by an interest in photography, family and local history and a fascination with Reece Winstone's Bristol books (produced many years ago prior to today's surge of interest in nostalgia). It was eventually Peter Daniels, a photographer and the author of several Salisbury books, who inspired me to 'get on with it'. My roots in Gillingham go back a long way! My great-great-great grandfather was married in St Mary's church in 1820 and all generations since, bar one, have been married in the same place. The average age of all my grandparents was ninety-nine, so I learnt a lot from their memories, an experience which helps when studying local history.

Gillingham is fortunate in that there were photographers around to record the people of the town and the many, often gradual, changes to the buildings, shops, etc. Adam Gosney and Charles Johnson were studio photographers up until the beginning of the twentieth century. When Edgar Samways used to run out of postcards, he popped out of his shop and took some fresh photographs, which he did right up until the 1930s. W. Phillips of East Stour was prolific with his plate camera, particularly in the Stour villages, whilst Ernest Berry's photos cover the 1930s and 1940s. It was around this time that cameras were developed for personal use – although the quality of Box Brownie photographs are not up to the standard of those taken by experts, such as Johnson, Samways and Berry. However, life was recorded and many of the results are represented in this book. At this point I shall issue a plea to those that are custodians of the family photos – please record the date, the event and names on the back. The memories fade rapidly, so do it now!

It has often been said to me that Gillingham is not a pretty place and certainly not a tourist attraction. Whilst it does not have as many historic and picturesque features as its close neighbour, Shaftesbury, it does have a great variety of architectural features for the discerning visitor to find. Unfortunately, two great fires in 1694 and 1742 destroyed over forty houses – who knows what great buildings were lost? However, the purpose of this collection is not to feature old buildings, such as Great House, the Malt House or the humps and hollows of King's

Court (one of King John's houses), but to concentrate on areas, such as the High Street. The virtue of this approach is that the reader can appreciate the changes and revel in nostalgia, with the added advantage of seeing the people who have lived and worked in the town and surrounding villages.

At the beginning of the seventeenth century, Gillingham was still a small village. The present High Street consisted of houses and dwellings of the period with at least two inns, the Red Lion and The Phoenix. The Free School was a large building near the church. Its most famous pupil was Edward Hyde, First Earl of Clarendon (1609-1674), who was the father of Queen Mary II and Queen Anne. Robert Frampton, who was later to become the Bishop of Gloucester, was elected headmaster of the school in 1648.

Despite its rural setting, Gillingham could claim to be an industrial town. In 1769, the Gillingham Silk Co. established the silk throwing industry (i.e., the process of preparing raw silk for the weaver). In the early years of the nineteenth century, around 160 people were employed in the mill itself. Girl apprentices were often obtained from London workhouses. In 1847, Oake Woods opened their bacon factory. The railway arrived in 1859, closely followed by the Gillingham Pottery, Brick and Tile Co. in 1865. A cattle and stock market developed and this was followed by the emergence of firms still existing today, i.e., Bracher Bros, J.H. Rose & Sons, Hudson & Martin, Lights and Sticklands. The population grew from 1,873 in 1801 to 3,380 in 1901.

During the first three decades of the twentieth century, the prosperity of the town continued. A market was held every other Monday and the calf market was the second largest in the country. There was a large dairy depot for manufacturing cheese and supplying milk to London, as well as Eden Shute's butter factory and Slade's mineral works. There was also the smell of Maloney's glue factory! After 1945 there was a steady decline and the end of the market in the 1950s seemed to mark the end of industrial Gillingham.

However, by the 1970s, the trend was reversing and new firms – such as Sherman Chemicals, Biokil, Sigma Aldrich, Wessex Fare, and Chester Jefferies – came to the town. Land was released for housing development and the town started to grow again, sadly without a reasonable infrastructure. However, the 'Relief Road' appeared in the late 1980s, following much controversy and disruption for traders. Le Neubourg Way (named after Gillingham's twin town in Normandy) provided the opportunity for a supermarket to be built. Reputed to be the third busiest Waitrose store in the country, it is now the focal point for the regeneration of the town's retail trade.

In the last ten years, the expansion of Gillingham has also included a huge building and refurbishment programme at the primary schools in School Road and at Milton and also Gillingham School (after the demolition of the old Grammar school). A new primary school was built at Wyke and the town has a new library and museum at Chantry Fields. The quality of education provided in the town has often been the driving force for families moving into the area, such that there is now serious discussion about building another primary school to meet the needs of the new population.

One thing is certain, Gillingham will continue to change and hopefully someone will continue to record those changes.

I hope you enjoy the book!

David Lloyd
1998

One
Around the Town

Chantry Bridge, 1950. This old footpath over the River Stour leads to Chantry Fields which, until 1993, was the only way to get to the two cottages beyond.

The Square from St Mary's church tower, 1966. Chantry Fields, at the top, is now the site of Waitrose and Le Neubourg Way.

The Square, c. 1911. Slade & Sons dominates this scene. W.E. Samways is the pharmacist and also the photographer for many of the different postcard scenes of the town at this time. The door to the left of Samways' shopfront is the entrance to the post office.

Slade and Sons, *c.* 1911. This department store opened in 1901. From left to right: Mary Slade, -?-, -?-, Bill Slade Snr, ? Bailey, Hubert Hillier, Bill Slade Jnr, -?-, Arthur Belgin.

High Street, 1960. The Grosvenor Arms' inn buildings, to the left, were demolished in 1996. The trees were part of The Vicarage's garden (now Rawson Court). The car park was built on land in the garden that was purchased by the council.

"The mill", Gillingham.

The Mill, 1922. The building on the far left, in the process of demolition, was the silk workrooms with the upper dormitory floor used to house the girl apprentices. To the right of it is the silk mill, where the silk was separated from the cocoons. The next part of the building was the grist mill, for the grinding of corn and wheat. The mill manager lived in the house to the right – which still survives. The mill, left derelict for several years, was finally destroyed by fire in 1982. The old waterwheel was bought by the owner of Waterloo Mill at Silton and now awaits restoration.

The Old Bridge Gillingham

The Town Bridge, late 1930s. This is the bridge that John Constable painted in 1823 (the original painting now hangs in the Tate Gallery). The Regal Cinema, on the left, opened in 1934.

J Herridge & Co., 1906. This was situated opposite Lloyds Bank where ShoeRack and Chantry TV are today.

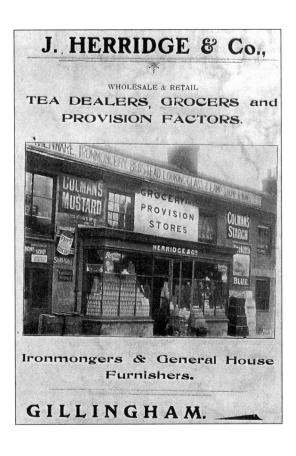

High Street, *c.* 1904. The building on the right was built from local brick for the Wilts & Dorset Bank in 1877. The bank's roots in the town go back to 1836, when Edward Neave was appointed agent. It was extended in the 1920s and, in 1941, was absorbed by Lloyds Bank.

Bowles' outfitters and hatters, High Street, c. 1911. From the 1920s until the late 1950s, this was Peach's tobacconists and hairdressers. It is now Gylla Galore.

A visit to the town in pony and trap, c. 1916. The children are Joan Lewis (back), Ann Hannam, Betty New and John Lewis. The Wilts & Dorset Bank (now Lloyds) is to the left in the background. The small gate led to 'Fernbank'.

High Street from the bottom of School Road, 1960. Parents congregate to meet their children from school. Mrs Robinson is in the car.

Stickland's ironmongers (on the left), 1920s. The business was started in 1882 by Edwin Roberts Stickland and was continued, until quite recently, by his great-grandson, Peter Crocker. The house to the far left was once owned by James Dunn, a seedsman, whose son later made his family a household name with Dunn's Seeds Ltd.

Junction of High Street, Newbury Road and Station Road, 1906. Stickland's are selling Shell petrol. The shop on the left is Strange's shoe shop.

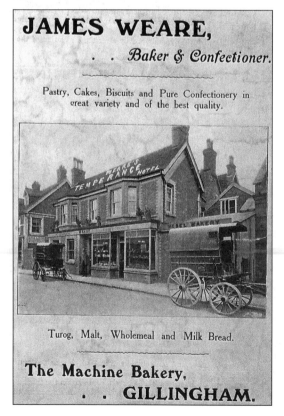

JAMES WEARE,

. . *Baker & Confectioner.*

Pastry, Cakes, Biscuits and Pure Confectionery in great variety and of the best quality.

Turog, Malt, Wholemeal and Milk Bread.

The Machine Bakery,

. . GILLINGHAM.

James Weare, baker and confectioner of Newbury, 1906. He also dispensed homeopathic medicines and kept a temperance hotel.

Peach's saloon, on the site now occupied
by Light's garage, 1907. Mr Peach
moved to the High Street in the 1920s.

Newbury, 1960. Mr Taplin was a chemist here for many years.

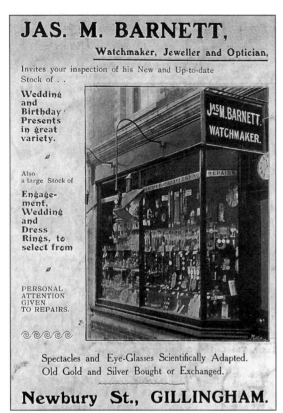

JAS. M. BARNETT,

Watchmaker, Jeweller and Optician,

Invites your inspection of his New and Up-to-date
Stock of . .

**Wedding
and
Birthday
Presents
in great
variety.**

Also
a large Stock of

**Engage-
ment,
Wedding
and
Dress
Rings, to
select from**

PERSONAL
ATTENTION
GIVEN
TO REPAIRS.

Spectacles and Eye-Glasses Scientifically Adapted.
Old Gold and Silver Bought or Exchanged.

Newbury St., GILLINGHAM.

Jas M. Barnett, watchmaker, jeweller
and optician of Newbury, 1906.

Light's garage, Newbury, 1950s. This was the first garage in Gillingham to have a pull-in
forecourt. Motorcycles were sold from the shop on the left. In the buildings behind the tanker
was Stone's greengrocery, followed by Bob Pester (prior to his move to Queen Street). The
capacity of the tanker shown is half that of modern day vehicles. Regent petrol was sold from
1949 until 1969, when it was taken over by Texaco.

Royal Hotel, Newbury, *c.* 1920. The garden to the left is now part of Bracher Bros.

Newbury on Market Day, 1904. Bracher Bros, established in 1866, moved to the middle building in 1896. They advertised themselves as cabinetmakers, house furnishers, decorators, painters, paperhangers, upholsterers and undertakers. Note the two lions on the front of the Royal – where's the missing one now?

Mrs George Jukes outside her cottage at Lodden, 1940s.

Duncliffe Wood today is one of the largest woods in North Dorset, sitting on the top of Duncliffe Hill, which looks across the Blackmore Vale and the Stour Valley towards Shaftesbury. The hill has probably been clothed in woodland since the retreat of the last ice sheet from Britain over 12,000 years ago. Past owners were King's College and the Forestry Commission. It was acquired by the Woodland Trust in 1985.

Police station and courthouse, School Road, *c.* 1905. It was built in 1890.

The fire station at the top of School Lane, 1935. This photograph shows brigade members with their Lincoln fire engine. From left to right, back row: J Hine, T. Hayden, T. Flower, A. Sheppard, A. Belgin. Centre row: E. Hine (driver), T. Hillier, J. Webber, H. Luffman, D. Tucker. Front row: H. Harris (captain), J. Burtt, J. Case, L. Brown.

Westminster Bank, 1925. The town's lecture hall was originally on this site but was demolished in 1900 to make way for the new bank premises of Messrs Stuckey & Co. The design was by G.H. Oakley, a Bristol architect. Construction costs were £4,449 (exclusive of sinking a well and providing office fittings). For a short while it was taken over by Parrs, until 1923, when it became the Westminster Bank. In 1970 this organisation merged with the National Provincial to become the National Westminster.

Interior of Westminster Bank, c. 1960. The manager at this time was Mr Shipp. Only half of the ground floor was used as office space. The remainder and upper floors were occupied by the incumbent manager.

Post office, Station Road, 1930s. Miss Lovelace is accompanied by Jack King and Charlie Stickland. Nicholsons, the printers, are to the right.

Station Road, *c.* 1915. The building to the left, formerly Miss Dunn's High School for girls, was being used at this time by the Red Cross. Indeed, it functioned as a hospital for the duration of the First World War. Afterwards, it became the National Provincial Bank and is now a Masonic lodge.

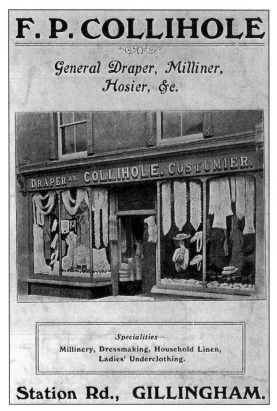

F. P. COLLIHOLE

General Draper, Milliner, Hosier, &c.

DRAPER AND COLLIHOLE, COSTUMIER.

Specialities—
Millinery, Dressmaking, Household Linen, Ladies' Underclothing.

Station Rd., GILLINGHAM.

F.P. Collihole, general draper in Station Road, 1906. These premises were later occupied by Ayles and Owen.

South Western Hotel, 1906. The proprietor at this time was George Bignal, who was to be the grandfather of Mary Bignal-Rand, the Olympic athlete. The hotel was used by commercial travellers that had arrived by rail. On market days, farmers and dealers parked their carts and carriages and hotel staff looked after the horses.

Brickyard, late 1960s. The Gillingham Pottery, Brick and Tile Co. was founded in 1865. The first two shareholders were John Williams Bell and Robert Sadler Freame, solicitors who played a major part in the future development of the town. The products of the brickyard were durable and of very good quality – as evidenced by many buildings in the locality. Pipes were made for agricultural drainage and such roof tiles are seen all over the South, in particular Bournemouth. The yard closed in 1968, when production became unprofitable.

Lime Tree House and The Barton, 1966. The Barton was occupied by Shephard Bros, tailors, for many years.

Queen Street from the church tower, 1966.

P. Stacey and Son, Queen Street, 1952. The board on the left advertises the programme for the Regal Cinema and the shop is decorated in preparation for the Queen's visit. Percy Stacey took over the hairdressers from Mr Cole in January 1948 and continued running the business until his death in 1970. His son, Ron, took over until 1984. The shop, next to The Smouldering Boulder, is now a private residence.

The Bay Store, *c.* 1905. Robert Lush was the proprietor. The field was common land in front of Lodbourne Farmhouse and was used by visiting funfairs and circuses until the early 1960s, when Lodbourne Green was built.

Peacemarsh Stores, late 1960s. This establishment was run by the Smith sisters.

Plank House and Wyke Street, 1960s. The house was used as a hospital during the First World War.

Wyke Road and Beehive cottage, 1930s. The cottage was demolished to make access to the new housing development via Coldharbour. Broad Robin field is to the right.

Marleaze, on the left, and Wyke Road, 1941. Lt Col. Charles Wallis lived in Wyke House (hidden by the trees on the far right). When the Local History Society was formed, in 1953, Col. Wallis was appointed honorary curator and was the driving force behind the society obtaining a museum, an ambition which was achieved in 1958. He was also the brother of Barnes Wallis, the famous inventor.

Wyke Road and maltsters' cottages, 1920s. Matthews' brewery is in the distance.

Wyke Hall, 1930s. Now restored and divided into flats, it was built by Richard de Wyke in the reign of Edward III and still has a minstrel gallery, oak panelling and some parts of the Tudor building. Before the Reformation it was, for a time, supposed to have been a monastery and the lake was presumably the monks' fish pond. During the Second World War, it was used to billet army doctors and nursing sisters.

Thorngrove House, Common Mead Lane, 1966. This Victorian house was once owned by Sir Harold and Lady Pelly. It was used during the Second World War as a billet for American officers and, afterwards, as a Dr Barnardo's childrens' home. Today, it is owned by Scope and is part of a horticultural work centre.

The Viaduct, 1920s. This is situated where the London to Exeter railway line crosses the Kington Magna road. Edgar Samways took this photograph.

Rolls Bridge Farm, 1929. All the fields of the farm are now developed for housing and only one of the original farm buildings remain.

General view of Gillingham, taken in 1929.

Two

Gillingham at Work

Workmen at Maloneys, Station Road, c. 1920.

Saddlery at Newbury, *c.* 1900. Mr George Gibbs Conway is the saddler and harness maker. The building is just to the right of the footpath down to the railway platform. Mr Read, and then Mr Ozzard – a tinsmith, occupied the site for many years after this photograph was taken.

'Jack' Ozzard of Newbury. Jack's father, William, ran his business from 1914, initially in Railway Terrace and then on Railway Bridge.

Len Fudge working with his lathe at the Rotary Works in Station Road, 1920s. The Lion Engine Co. was one of many enterprises run by Charlie Maloney and produced small engines, which were used by farmers nationally as well as in developing countries. One surviving example of these engines can be seen in the Museum.

Three generations of the Ozzard family – Jack, William and Roy – at their workshop in Newbury, 1950s.

Milmer Brown, postman, 1900. He was also verger at St Mary's church for forty-four years.

Harry Case, *c.* 1920. The tins of biscuits were supplied by McVitie & Price and W. & R. Jacob & Company.

Hudson & Martin staff at the sawmills in Station Road, 1924. This was on the site now occupied by Sherman Chemicals. The sawmills closed in 1960.

Oil Agency staff at the brickyard depot, late 1950s. From left to right: Billy Dennett, Bill Andrews, ? White, Mickey Martin, -?-, Jim ?, Harry Hunt.

Harry Allard and his pigs at Lodden Farm, 1920s. Harry's children in the background are, from left to right: Bert, Joe and Jack.

Farmer Pitman at Culvers. His son, Vic, is on the back of the tractor and the children are probably from the Collis family.

Sawing wood at Springfield, Bugley, 1915. This was owned by the Hannam family at this time.

Mr A. Francis controls the horses at harvest time, Cole Street Farm, late 1940s.

Bob Pester, greengrocer, 1956. He was well known in the area from his grocery round and he is pictured here in Fairey Crescent with Joan Dear and her children: Terry, Raymond and Rosalyn.

Geoff Kite on deliveries. He and his family were fishmongers in the town for many years with a shop in the High Street, which is now occupied by the Abbey Friar.

Fred Proudley, hardware merchant. The business was started in the late 1920s by Fred's father, John, in the Old Forge at Peacemarsh.

Proudley's van, late 1950s. Fred's son, Eric, still continues a van service today in Gillingham and the surrounding villages.

London Central Meat Co., near the church gate, High Street, 1935. The site is now occupied by 'Scenes'.

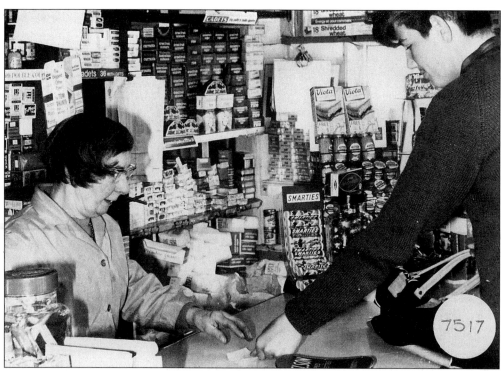

Miss Smith serves Barry Young at Peacemarsh Stores, *c.* 1967.

Oake Woods, Station Road, 1963. T.A. James, the manager (right), and the sales manager, Jack Stone, discuss sales matters as a van is being loaded at the factory.

The Wiltshire cutting line at Oake Woods, 1963. On the left are: Vic Lane, Cecil Coombes, Frank Hutchinson, Taff Pritchard, Bob Vowles, Roger Lydford, Gid Stone. On the right: Stan Randall, Dusty Millard, Bob Smith, Butch Harris (hidden), Art Butt, Gid Stone.

Ballast cleaning on the track just past Railway Terrace, 1966. British Rail staff include Ted Lankey, George Bealing, Cliff Lloyd, Inspector Tolley, Fred Hopkins, Bill Fishley and Mervyn Biss. The machinery was Swiss made and the task involved a twenty-four hour operation on a Sunday.

Tommy Suttle and Nurse Read, The Pharmacy, The Square, late 1960s. Tommy took over from Ernest Samways in 1964 and continued until his retirement in 1988. The shop is now known as St Mary's Pharmacy. Nurse Read was the district nurse and midwife for about thirty years.

Three
Church and Chapel

St Mary's church. The *Domesday Book* records that the church was granted by William the Conqueror to the Abbey of Shaftesbury. The oldest part of the present building is the chancel, built in the Decorated style (1270-1370). The medieval nave was demolished in 1838 and rebuilt by the Revd Henry Deane, vicar of the church from 1832 until 1882.

Interior of St Mary's church, 1905. The galleries, upper left and right, were removed in 1918. This reduced the seating capacity but the added light and improved appearance of the church more than compensated for this loss.

The Vicarage, Queen Street, 1907. This building dates from 1883, but there has been a residence for the incumbent on this same site from the institution of the first vicar in 1318. In the time of Canon John Fisher, the painter John Constable (1770-1837), his friend, was a visitor. From 1916, the curates were expected to live in The Vicarage.

Bird's eye view of The Vicarage and gardens, 1966. The garden once extended to the river, with the lower part used for vegetable growing (now the car park) and the upper part utilized for the annual church fête. Both the building and the garden are now incorporated into Rawson Court.

Nativity scene in St Mary's church, *c.* 1950. From left to right are: Michael Rose, Susan Raymond, Mary Brickell, Dennis Hannam, Lyn Light, Bob Carter. The identity of the girls kneeling down is uncertain.

Sister Hart and her Bible class, photographed in the playground of the original Wyke School, 1944. From left to right, back row: Margaret Cox, Brenda Scammell, Dorothy Gray, Alwyn Case, Kitty Perrot, Eileen Cross, Joyce King, Pat Francis. Front row: Ruth Martin and Sister Hart.

Interior of the Catholic church, Cemetery Road, c. 1925. The church was converted from two cottages given by the Freame family and dedicated to St Benedict. The church was destroyed by fire in September 1929 and was rebuilt, and then later enlarged, in 1952 and 1976.

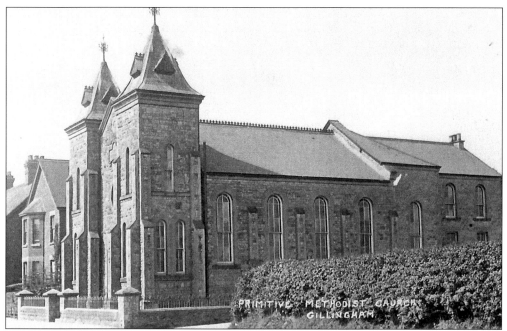

Primitive Methodist church, Queen Street. This was built in 1876 to replace the original 1836 church in Turners Lane (now a private residence). The Queen Street Society, as they became known, operated independently to the High Street Weslyans until 1963, when the Queen Street church was closed. It was subsequently taken over by the Royal Yachting Association, which had links in the town for many years, and is now owned and used by 'Materialize'.

Revd F. Adams outside the old Baptist church, Newbury, 1950s. The building was demolished in 1970.

Helpers at the Methodist church. Ruth Welch, Kath Rose, -?-, Kath Rawlins, -?-, Doris Welch, -?-, Addie Bracher, -?-.

Methodist Sunday School. On the far left are Doris Welch and Joyce Drewitt.

Four
View of the Villages

Milton on Stour, 1930s. The blacksmith's house is facing the camera and the forge was on the other side. Freddie Vincent, the blacksmith, made the porch to the adjoining house on the left. This was where Samuel Braddick once lived before he moved into Station Road.

Bob England's store and post office at Milton, late 1930s.

The Kendalls, Milton. This was the home of Blandford and Ina Matthews (of GB Matthews' brewery) in the 1970s.

Spicketts Farmhouse opposite Milton church, 1950s. The house is 200 years old and was formerly held by the Matthews family. For the past 100 years it has been occupied by three generations of the Knapton family. Unusual features of the building include the wrought-iron verandahs and the inwardly-opening windows.

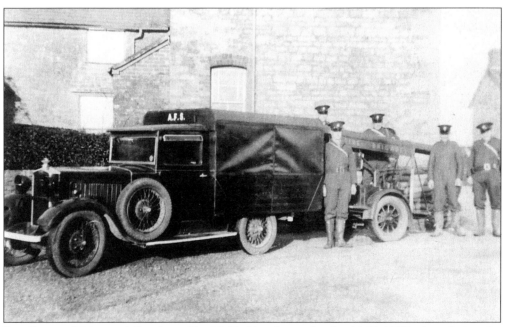

East Stour vehicle specially adapted by Mr Budden for use by the Air Raid Wardens during the Second World War.

Arthur Farthing, engineer at Hindleys', Bourton, 1915. Arthur travelled the whole country on behalf of the company and this photograph was used on publicity material.

Hindleys' workshop, c. 1915. This is part of the erecting shops for the high-speed gas engines.

Waterwheel at Hindleys' works. Built in 1837, this wheel was reputed to be the largest in England.

Workers at Hindleys' Bourton foundry.

The Elsworth twins on the shell case, 1930s. This was on the triangle of green (now gone) at West Stour, a popular place for children to play or take car numbers. The girls are facing the road to the church and the A30 runs behind them.

The Trim family of West Stour, 1900. Eden Trim with children Charlie, May and Roland. The photograph was taken by Charles Johnson of Gillingham.

The Burgess family at West Stour, *c.* 1900. From left to right: Charles, George, Mr Burgess, Margaret, Olive, Mrs Burgess, Sid and Lucy.

Sunday School gathering at West Stour, *c.* 1900. The medals were given for regular attendance and good conduct.

Farmworkers at Manor Farm, West Stour, 1911. From left to right: Mr Burgess, Walter Lloyd and George Wetherall.

West Stour School group with teacher Mrs Gray, *c.* 1920. Fourth from the left in the back row is Miss Gibbs (infant teacher), whilst on her left is Vida Lloyd. From left to right, front row: -?-, ? Cox, Christina Lloyd, ? Gray, ? Gray, ? Flower and Harold Cox (who later married Christina)

Harry Lloyd at West Stour, 1911. The brass head of the ceremonial stave is decorated with a ship design, probably linked to the Ship Inn, and was used on special occasions of the East and West Stour and Fifehead Magdalen Club (founded in 1762). Harry was well known in the village for his garland making and leading the club's walks.

Coronation celebrations at West Stour, 1911. The Ship Inn is in the background. The marquee was supplied by Hudson & Martin of Gillingham and Harry Lloyd is holding his stave and garland in the back row.

Mr Wetherall at Highbridge Mill, East Stour, *c.* 1920. The vehicle on the left was registered in the name of William Wetherall and is described in registration records as a black, twenty-horsepower, one ton truck.

Highbridge Mill, East Stour. Powered by the River Stour, the mill ground locally-grown barley and wheat into flour for pigs. It went out of use at the beginning of the twentieth century.

East Stour Home Guard, 1940s.

The Stours Orchestra, 1930s. This organisation was founded in East Stour by C.E. Davies, a former London orchestra musician. From left to right, back row: Sidney Compton, Joe Fowles, George Harris, Walter Morgan. Middle row: Fred Fowles, ? Brickell, A. Maidment, C.E. Davies, Dan Tucker, Taylor Jones, G. Fowles, Charlie Marvin. Front row: Mrs Davies, Celia Fowles, Mrs H. Butler, Mrs Dick Veal, Charlie Raymond, Wilfred Gibbons.

The Vicarage, Fifehead Magdalen. This building was described in the Historical Monuments survey (of 1972) as having two storeys, rubble walls – in part rendered, with ashlar dressings – and a thatched roof. It is probably of seventeenth-century origin with eighteenth-century alterations and enlargement. It is now a private residence.

Fifehead House, Fifehead Magdalen. Demolished in 1964, it possessed three storeys, with ashlar walls and slate-covered roofs. It was built in 1807 to replace the Tudor manor that stood there.

Threshing at Middle Farm, Fifehead Magdalen, 1941.

Carpenters' workshop at Stour Row in 1903. The workers are, from left to right (probably): James Kiddle, Bill Hull, Bert Pike, Jimmy Pike and Jimmy Pike Snr.

Cockerell's bakery and shop, Kington Magna, *c.* 1911.

Kington Magna School group, 1954/55. From left to right: John Highnam, Donald Hinks, Nigel Dyke, Robert Counsell, Robin Draycott, Stan Chard, Pat Osborne, David Evans (headmaster). Middle row: Douglas Dyke, Nicholas Hopkins, Philip Arnold, David Draycott, Malcolm Bullen, Christopher Mason, Gerald Hinks. Front row: Susan Tutcher, Brenda Wareham, Yvonne Higgins, Beverly Evans, Angela Tutcher, Pauline Bennett.

Charlie Ash and Keith Richards take a break from their groom duties at the National Stud, Sandley, October 1964. One month later, the Stud moved its headquarters to Newmarket.

Kington Magna and Buckhorn Weston Home Guard, c. 1942. From left to right, back row: Ernie Hibbs, Cecil Crew, Claude Sennick, Eric Dowding, Stan Cox, Phil Perrett, Arthur Beale. Middle row: Burnice Lewis, -?-, -?-, Len Dowding, George Dowding, -?-, -?-, -?-. Front row: Harry Wareham, -?-, Arthur Arnold, Bert Foyle, Les Cockerell, Percy Cox, Bert Cox Jnr, Percy Newport

The family of Thomas and Edith Arnold and their six children (and Benny the dog) at Bowden, Kington Magna, *c.* 1926. From left to right, back row: Harry, Bessie (Hallett), Jack, Jim. Front row: Mabel (Kendall), Thomas, Edith (née Hayward), Mary (Lewis).

Kington Magna Women's Institute, 1950s. From left to right, back row: Mrs Irene Arnold, Mrs J. Stokes, Mrs Linda Dowding, Miss Daisy Gillett, Mrs A. Hoskins, Mrs Brenda Evans. Front row: Mrs E. Hayter, Miss Caddy, Mrs P. Cox, Miss P. Reynolds, Mrs S. Wall.

Kington Magna football team and supporters, 1956. From left to right, back row: Mary Feltham, Bert Cox Jnr, Mrs Owen Shaw, Bert Cox Snr, Tom Arnold, Jack Osborne, Tony Osborne, Ron Luffman, Ernie Stokes, Horst Schroeder, Frank Galleymore, Frank Curtis, Jack Watts, Fred Osborne, Revd Frank Edwards, Fred Bateman, -?-, Irene Arnold. Front row: Cecil Crew, Bob Underdown, Geoff Dowding, Dick Arnold, Owen Shaw, Bob Holly, George Baumgarten, Fred Crew, Arthur Arnold. Sitting, cross-legged: George Osborne, Ray Crew.

Kington Magna church choir, mid-1950s. From left to right, back row: Chris Highnam, Bill Reynolds, Tom Arnold, David Evans Jnr, Daisy Gillett, Bertie Read, Evelyn Raymond, Bill Dowding, David Evans Snr, Geoff Dowding, Clarence Dowding. Front row: Philip Arnold, Esme Spenn, Brenda Wareham, Doreen Hanham, Ruth Goodship, Joyce Dowding, Yvonne Higgins, Dianne Arnold, Doreen Drake.

Milkers at Manor Farm, Silton. These workers would have used traditional hand-milking methods.

A milker at Manor Farm with his 'modern' equipment.

Former pupils at the centenary celebrations of Woodville School, Stour Provost. A boarding school (mixed) with a residence for a master was built in 1850. From left to right, back row: John Cox, Mrs Edith Farthing, Arthur Maidment, Mrs Mabel Lloyd. Front row: Mrs Lockyer, Mrs Alice Martin, Charlie Pike, Mrs Ralph. Edith Farthing (née Beale) is recorded in the school's records of June 1894 as being away ill 'with inflammation of lung hardly expected to pull through it'.

Milk delivery, c. 1910. The name on the cart is George Fricker, of Huntingford.

Blackmore Vale Hunt at the Stapleton Arms, Buckhorn Weston

Empire Day at Buckhorn Weston School, c. 1903.

Five

Transport

Walter Hunt with two of P.O. Baker's Model-T cars, 1920s. Baker's started in business in 1912.

Mrs Agnes Bell, as photographed by Adam Gosney of Sherborne, c. 1882. Mrs Bell, the mother of John Williams Bell, solicitor, died 4 September 1886, aged ninety-four years. She was obviously a well-respected person as, on her funeral day, nearly all the houses were veiled and the shops closed from Knapp House to the church. The bier was preceded by the gentlemen of the town, with most of the leading tradesmen following behind.

Mabel Beale with her bicycle, 1902. Magnet bicycles, such as this one, were manufactured in Gillingham by Light's of Newbury. W. Phillips of East Stour took this photograph.

E.J. Wiles' horse and van, *c.* 1930. The bakery was in Hardings Lane.

W.E. Butler's railway delivery wagon.

Sidney Hannam with his four-horsepower BSA and sidecar, *c.* 1920. This was purchased from E.R. Stickland of Gillingham. The passengers are daughters, Ann and Martha.

Sid Kite on deliveries, 1910. William Kite was fishmonger, fruiterer and licensed dealer in game.

Wiles, coal merchants, operated from Peacemarsh and the station yard in the 1950s. Mr Hardcastle and Mr Chandler were the coalmen.

Michael Rose with Braddicks' lorry and tractor, 1952. The tractor was being collected from Doncaster to be supplied to Gordon Pickford of Stourton.

Matthews and Co. Austin lorry, *c.* 1950. The Matthews family operated from their brewery in Wyke for about 200 years, until they sold out to Hall and Woodhouse in 1963. The brewery used a buffalo as a trade mark.

Ruth Welch and Jean Ayles of Hunt's Dairies, New Road, 1960s.

S. Braddick & Son, Station Road, 1950s. Samuel Braddick originally started up in business as a blacksmith at Milton. When he started dealing in farm machinery, in 1917, he moved to Station Road. The buildings shown are now fronted by the Rover garage.

J.H. Rose & Sons's Austin lorry, 1956. The firm was started by John Henry Rose in 1889, with a borrowed horse and cart, and hauled coal from Radstock. By its centenary year, the firm employed twenty staff, ran around twenty vehicles and could boast a turnover of £1,000,000.

Battle of Britain AA Command engine 34049 prepares to pull a train loaded with horses. This was a result of the National Stud transferring from Sandley to Newmarket in 1964. The boxes came from all over the Southwest and it took a week to establish the train.

Issetta bubble car made by BMW and owned by Phil Bland, local insurance agent, pictured here with his daughter, Carola, in 1962.

Six

Wartime Gillingham

Milmer Brown, the church verger, looks on as Mr Toogood and Sid Court remove the railings for the war effort. Mrs Court ran a scrapyard at Kingscourt.

Mr Jukes proudly displays his uniform at his house in Lodden during the First World War.

Women's Volunteer Service canteen workers, Second World War. The group includes: Mrs Thorne, Mrs Perrett, Mrs Hurley, Mrs Stocker, Mrs White, Mrs Stevens and Mrs Coward.

Mrs Court at Kingscourt during the Second World War. Apart from dealing in scrap, she was obviously in the market for other commodities – but no luck on this occasion!

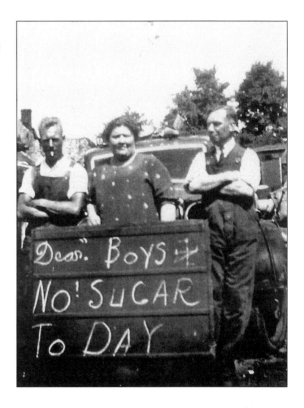

Royal Observer Corps, Second World War. From left to right, back row: A. Allard, C. White, R. Wadman. Middle row: H. Wiles, J. Herridge, M. Roberts, G. Jaggard, W. Tooze, G. Stone. Front row: H. Martin, ? Jukes, J. Scammell, E. Jukes. A post was set up near the football field and manned throughout the war, plotting all the German formations that raided Bristol.

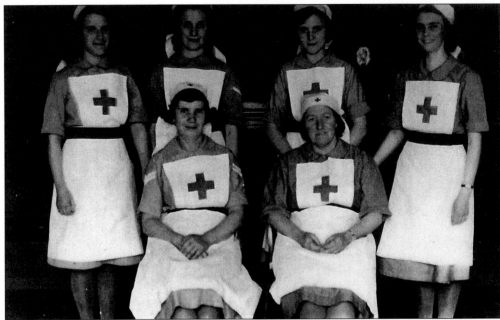

Red Cross group at the end of the Second World War. From left to right, back row: Eileen Cross, Joan Burt, Yvonne Ringh, Sheila Coombes. Front row: Rita Palmer, Mrs Victor Wadman.

Civil Defence first aid post at Newbury, Second World War. From left to right, back row: -?-, S. Strange, ? Coombes, C. Dicker. Middle row: Mrs Wadman, Hilda Collier, Mrs Scovell, Mrs Doris Johnston, -?- (evacuee), Miss Down, Mrs Edwards, Mrs Deam, Miss Bishop, Mrs Beaton, Miss Coombes, Mrs Jaggard, Mrs Molly Griffiths. Front row: Joan Walters (evacuee), Mrs Freda Howe, Miss B. Bracher, Mrs Buckley, Ivy Hiscock, Dorothy Brickell, Mrs Dickenson.

Private Lloyd CW 5726668, 4th Battalion, Dorset Regiment, 43 Wessex Division, 1940. Cliff and many of the local lads were members of the volunteer Territorial (or 4th Battalion). Called up at the outbreak of the Second World War, most of the war years were spent in coastal areas of Britain. In 1944, the 4th Battalion were involved in Operation Market Garden in Holland. This was a complex and daring attempt to capture the river crossings near Arnhem to cover the evacuation of the 1st Airborne. Under constant enemy fire, only 300 Dorsets survived the crossing, but 2,400 paratroopers were ferried back. Although Cliff survived, he was captured and spent the remainder of the war as a POW.

Threshing gang, 1941. R. Pitman and L. Trim with the Land Girls evacuated from Barrett's sweet factory in London.

Charles Brown, RAMC, 1941. By December 1940, there were three General Hospital Units in Gillingham (numbers 37, 55 and 56). All of these went out to West Africa during May and June of 1941. Doctors and medical officers were billeted in the Lodbourne area and the nursing sisters at Wyke Hall.

Air Training Corp 932 Flight at the grammar school, 1940. From left to right, back row: -?-, ? Taylor, R. Cullingford, -?-, J. Garrett, A. Jukes, D. Chislett, P. White, J. Bracher, P. Flower, D. King, J. Gale, K. Stokes, W. Burchell. Middle row: L. Tanswell, D. Waring, P. West, -?-, D. Lawley, -?-, J. Morgan, J. Case, -?-, H. Mathias, E. Hunt, A. Taylor, R. Taylor, R. Lydford. Front row: P. Gale, A. Southgate, S. Ford, P. Webber, ? Ford, C. Ford, C. Howe, R.V. Best, F/Lt Hurley, G. Guard, R. Whitmarsh, L. Hooper, R. Gray, T. Arnold, P. Steele, D. Hanham. Seated: -?-, B. Stokes, -?-, ? Lawrence, P. Bland, C. Read, E. Sage, K. Harcourt, R. Doggrell, J. Heal.

Sgt C.W. Brooks 31352268 of Company 'A', 277th Combat Engineer Battalion, US Army. Sgt Brooks was one of many American soldiers who camped in Gillingham during 1944, prior to the D-Day landings in France.

Royal Army Medical Corps vehicle, 1941. The RAMC used Gillingham as a mobilising centre and, although the size of the units is uncertain, most were usually equipped and staffed to run 600 beds and had around sixteen medical officers and fifty nursing sisters.

Mr Albert Harrison, ARP warden, 1940s. Mr Harrison was the manager of the Co-op store in Queen Street from 1919 until the mid-1950s. He was on various committees and was treasurer of the town band for twenty-five years.

ATC group at *HMS Dipper*, Henstridge Aerodrome, *c.* 1942. The plane in the background is a Seafire, the naval version of the Spitfire. From left to right, back row: Mervyn Biss, Ted Hunt, A. Arnold, M. Cross, Ken Dukes, ? Smith, M. Davis, Ivor Scammell. Third row: Ian Nicholson, R. Galbally, John Light, Norman Brickell, Ken Jukes, ? Avery, Stan Hine, C. Palmer. Second row: ? Snook, Ken Taylor, Ted Hardy, A. Lawrence, A. Fry, J. Fulcher, Ron Bristow, John Burgess. Front row: Phil Francis, S. Ford, P. White, RNAS Officer, W. Hurley (Commanding Officer), Brian Hurley, Ray Lydford, Laurie Hull, P. Gale.

Seven

Schooldays

GILLINGHAM.

A NATIONAL SCHOOL for Girls and Boys, will be shortly opened at the new School Room, near the Vicarage.

All the children will be taught reading, writing, summing, and knitting; and the girls will be taught needle-work.

Each child will pay one penny a week.

No child can be admitted under six years old; nor any who does not know the alphabet.

Parents wishing to send their children to this School, are requested to call at the Vicarage any morning between eight and ten o'clock.

August, 1839.

Neave, Printer, Gillingham.

National School notice, as distributed by Revd Henry Deane, vicar of St Mary's.

St Martin's Priory School in Queen Street, 1933.

County Primary School in School Road. Opened in 1875 and known as the Board School, it had an infant section and separate sections for boys and girls. This photograph was taken on 8 May 1977. Some days later, the buildings to the left and centre were devastated by fire. The school was rebuilt and the building on the right was retained and, in 1997, extended and incorporated into yet another new building as part of a major re-development scheme to cater for Gillingham's growing school population.

Class at County Primary School, late 1920s. From left to right, back row: ? Stone, Hilda Harrison, Miss Burt, Joan Coward, Jessica Hussey, Arthur Read. Second row: Joyce Rideout, Ivy Hiscock, Cyril Rowsell, Beryl Luffman, Len King. Third row: Ethel Hiscock, Molly Goodsen, Joan Flower, Mabel Miles, Phil Read. Front row: Eric Mansfield, Harry Whatley, Claude Street, Jack Read, Alice Thick.

County Primary choir, 1935. From left to right, back row: Marion Batts, Elsie Alner, Vera Gray, Mabel Miles, Gwen Stone, Ivy Hiscock. Middle row: Alice Thick, Joan Coward, Joan Flower, Myrtle Green, Joyce Burden, Jessica Hussey, Joyce Ridout, Kathleen Warr, Marjorie Setter, Beryl Luffman, Winnie Burden, Dorothy Kingham. Front row: -?-, -?-, Dorothy Welstead, Miss Stiling, Eileen Larcombe, Margaret Mansfield, -?- .

Mr Alfred Knott and the County Primary football team, 1935. From left to right: Mr Knott (trainer), R. Light, L. Gatehouse, R. White, A. Bullen, R. Harris, W. Andrew (manager). Front row: A. Read, C. Street, Cecil Collis, Percy Alger and Ron Hussey. Mr Locke was the headmaster at this time and Mr Knott and Mr Andrews were the only teachers at the school.

County Primary, c. 1950. Miss Jean Walker (who later married George Joyce) takes advantage of good weather to hold her class in the playground. The pupils are, from left to right: -?-, -?-, Chris Harding, Keith Francis, -?-, Robin Sadler, Peter Trowbridge, Janette Bird, Rosemary Hardcastle and Maureen Gatehouse. In the background, to the left, is Murial Allard's car.

County Primary class of 1959. From left to right, back row: Richard Gwilt, Robin Chard, Richard Lush, -?-, John Green, Roger Chant, Peter Cornford, Alan Whitehead, -?-, Peter Collis. Middle row: -?-, Elizabeth Higgin, Moira Green, Susan Bland, Noelle Francis, Elizabeth Stainer, Sally Trainor, Janice Hinson, Christine Coward, Nicola Hughes, Beryl Bashford, Christine Cadman. Front row: Christine Hatch, Beatrice Conway, Olivia Green, Cathy Kite, Sue Perry, Jane Greenstock, -?-, Ann Evans, Marion Bridle, Jill Gray, Angela Maidment, Linda Read.

Mr Dowse and the football team at County Primary, 1957. From left to right, back row: Ken Hardcastle, Richard Watts, Malcolm Jaggard, Mr Dowse, Bernard Gatehouse, David Ayles, Geoff Peters. Front row: Roy Palmer, Ian Maidment, John Betteridge, Roger Griffiths, Ian McQueen, Tim Suter.

Carey Camp, Wareham, 1959. This facility is still used by schools today, but is now known as the Carey Outdoor Education Centre. From left to right, back row: Miss Corbin, Michael Hicks, David Brewer, Graham Hughes, Michael Chant, David Brown, Roy Whitehead, Andrew Dunn, David Lloyd, Graham Hacker, Mr Trickett (headteacher). Front row: A.Yeatman, Sheila Davison, Carol Read, Ann Jaggard, Anne Denslow, Jackie Rice, Nesta Legg, Carol Sheppard, Shirley Flower, Mary Bridle, ? Cross, ? Yeatman, Erika Bland.

Mr Gwilt's class at County Primary School, 1967. From left to right, back row: Paul Luffman, Keith Manning, Douglas Knox, Keith Weeks, Geoffrey Yeatman, Simon Gay, Colin Gay. Middle row: Tony Sorrell, John Hodgson, Robert Koch, Jane Newcombe, Lyn Sorrell, Pam Philips, Dereck King, Lawrence Green, Rodney Drewitt. Front row: Amanda Biss, Rachel Suttle, Anette Ivy, Penny Abbot, Isla Palmer, Susan Lowry, Claire Luffman, Margret Philips, Hilary Birchall, Anita Scott.

Secondary Modern School, 1951. Built just before the Second World War, near to the Grammar School, the new school was at first occupied by pupils from the local primary school, to prevent the building being used as army billets. After the war, comprehensive education was discussed and argued for many years until finally, in 1959, the Secondary Modern and Grammar Schools merged. The buildings now form part of the newly extended and refurbished Gillingham School.

Secondary Modern School class, c. 1950. From left to right, back row: J. Osbourne, D. Curtis, D. Topp, M. Jones, I. Perry, P. Curtis, T. Cull, D. Hunt, D. Burton, J. Perrin. Third row: P. Hillier, ? Hanham, D. Gray, ? Boswell, M. Pike, R. Barter, P. Baumber, T. Harris, R. Bird, P.Dawe. Second row: D. Collis, P. Perrot, J. Stokes, J. Ralph, R. White, J. Ralph, D. Stone. Front row: G. Parsons, P. Target, J. Chalke, R. Frampton, P. Clarke, D. Adams, B. Mead, P. Thompson.

Grammar School, 1894. Founded in 1516 and known as The Free School until the new Gillingham Grammar School was officially opened in 1876.

Grammar School cricket team, 1894.

Grammar School prefects, 1894.

Typical Grammar School classroom at the turn of the twentieth century.

Swimming in the River Shreen at Bay, 1894. This was a popular spot for all local children, being shallow and safe to swim in. The school acquired its own baths in 1912 (off Bay Lane). During excavations for the pool, an ancient gravel bed was revealed and a series of oak posts was found, along with other evidence of a Neolithic lake-dwellers settlement dating from about 2500 BC.

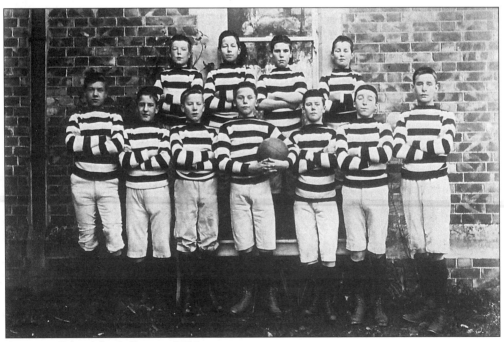

Grammar School football team, 1894.

Bicycle racing on Sports Day at the Secondary Modern School, 1958

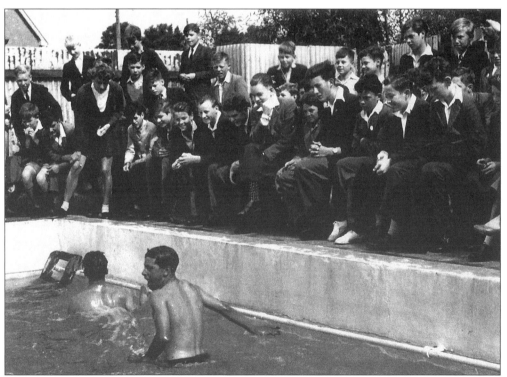

Boys from the Secondary Modern School enjoying Swimming Sports Day, 1958. Ken Hardcastle is in the water and Miss Calendar is giving encouragement.

Pat Chamberlain entered the Grammar School in 1941 and is pictured here in her new uniform. She returned to school in 1954 as a member of the teaching staff and eventually became senior mistress and then deputy head in the subsequent comprehensive school. When the governors agreed to admit girls to the school in 1916 they pronounced that '...all girls are required to wear a straw hat and the school hatband'.

Grammar School drive, 1941. The cricket pavilion was built in 1923 by the old boys of the school as a memorial to those of their comrades who had died in the First World War.

The last group of Grammar School teachers, Summer 1959. From left to right, back row: Mrs Jaggard (bursar), Mr Griffiths, Mr Evans, Mrs Easterbrook, Miss Westwood, Mr Hartley, Mr Jones, Mrs Esposito, Miss M. Scott, Miss E. Smith, Miss S. Appleby. Front row: Mr Yelling, Mr Hicks, Mr Hurley, Miss Chamberlain, Mr Webster (head), Mr Wagner, Mr Best, Mr Hunt, Mr Elphick.

The Grammar School's production of A Midsummer's Night Dream, December 1954. From left to right, back row: Gillian Ward, John Flashman, Clarence Dowding, Mark Loader, ? Taylor, -?-, David Stone, Margaret Hanham, David Trickett, Tom Vernon (now of Fat Man on a Bicycle fame), David Hopkins, Leonard Cowley, Sam Woodcock, Veronica Cowell. Front row: Anne Foulds, Wendy Few, Alan Rogers, Heather Cutler, Walters, Bridget Gantley, Janet Woods, Ivy Cox, June Collins.

Pat Chamberlain presents a retirement gift to Walter Edwin Hurley after a forty-four year long teaching career at Gillingham. He was described as a 'great schoolmaster, scientist and sportsman'. He was also well known for his singing and acting abilities.

Mr Hurley and his wife are guests of honour at a presentation dinner and dance to celebrate his retirement. 180 guests attended, representing the governing body, staff and old boys and girls.

Gillingham School Army Cadet Force, 1964. From left to right, back row: -?-, Mike Hicks, Robert Jordan, Kenny Oliver, David Jeans, David Cooper, Ian Norris. Middle row: Peter Stainer, Steve Guppy, Mike Chant, Bruce Cook, Bob Gristwood. Front row: George Flower, Peter Wells, -?-, Capt. Neil, N. Hawkswell, Nigel Forward, -?-.

Wyke School pupils, 1926. From left to right, back row: Miss Foot, -?-, Mark Fry, -?-, Ron Davies, -?-. Middle row: Herbert Green, ? Gould, Stella Doggrell. Front: -?-, -?-, Joyce Collis, Tom Fry, Roy Green, -?- and Kath Collis. The original school was built in 1890 at the junction of Wyke road and Lydfords Lane.

Miss Margaret Kirkham (deputy head) and Mrs Angela Dawson (teacher) open the gates at the newly-built Wyke Primary School in Deane Avenue for the first seventy-five pupils, 4 September 1991. Baroness Cox, the deputy speaker of the House of Lords, officially opened the school, built to take 210 pupils, on 22 November 1991.

Eight
Life and Leisure

Camping in Chantry Fields, *c.* 1913. The sign on the tent says 'Back to the Land'. From left to right, back row: -?-, Ted Hiscock, A. Hussey, C. Parfitt, G. Broomfield, T. Foot. Front row: W. Edwards, A. Burton, S. Smith.

Harold Reed relaxing at Oakleigh, Wyke, 1908

North Dorset election, 1906.

The ornate Edwardian mantelpiece
at Oakleigh, Wyke, 1908

Eliza Stickland seated at the piano
with family and friends at
Oakleigh, Wyke, 1908

The Lumsden Lambs (members of the Bible class club named after Revd Lumsden) football team. Matches were played in Chantry Fields. From left to right, back row: Billy Edwards, Edgar Green, Gus Broomfield, C. Stickland, ? Harris. Front row: Bert Hiscock, -?-, Percy Lodge, Bill Coward, Stanley Coward.

Territorial football team, 1921/1922 season. The team were winners of the Dorset Team Challenge Cup. From left to right, back row: Cpl A.S. Musselwhite, R. Dukes, S. Bowden, J.R. Algar, Sgt Instr. W.A. Slocombe. Middle row: H.C. Luffman, Sgt W.E. Edwards, W.V. White, H.B. Flower, R. Elcock. Front row: R.H. White, F. Broomfield, H. Francis, T. Marsh, E.P. Hooper.

Town football club, 1938/39 season. From left to right, back row: Charlie Gray, Fred Case, Harry Collarbone, Mr Drake, Mr Beaton, Arthur Shephard, Reg Gray, Bill Miles. Next row (standing): Bert Rose, Jim Maidment, Ken Harris, Roy George, John Harkness. Third row: Eric White, 'Jock' Trainer, George Maidment, Frank Lane. Second row (seated): Bert Collis, Glyn Lawley, Ted Duffett. Front row: George Collis, Ron Frances, Vic Lovell, Fred White.

Town football club, 1966. From left to right, back row: Fred Brown, Maurice Hannam, Derek Martin, Gerald White, Chris Vassie, Dave Parsons, Ken Warren, Tommy Whiffen, 'Dinger' Bell, Mick Osborne, Mr Hine, Terry Lush. Front row: Ray Crew, Brian Flower, Peter Riglar, Len Arney, Gordon Luffman.

Gillingham Agricultural Show, 1913. Herb Gibbs, from Cole Street Farm, with Violet and her foal, winning first prize. Ted Duffett and his family ran the farm.

Gillingham Agricultural Show, 1920s. Harry Dufosee, Harry Allard and Jim Bastable are in the photograph.

Gillingham Agricultural Show, 8 September 1913. These shows were held at Lodden Farm, where the football pitch is today.

Market day in Station Road, 1930s.

The wedding day of Kit Stickland and Charles Reed, pictured at Oakleigh, Wyke, 1909.

Wedding of Reg Budgen to Hilda Martin at Queen Street Methodist church, 1932. From left to right, back row: Phoebe Martin, Rose Martin, Jack Burt (best man), Dollie Martin, Pearl Coward, Hannah Myall, -?-, Reg Martin and Nellie Hiscock with Ken and Doris. Front row: Mr and Mrs Budgen, Ivy Hiscock, Reg Budgen, Hilda Martin, Joyce Martin, Kate Martin, Tom Martin.

Wartime wedding of Fred Martin and his
bride, 1942.

Wedding group at the South Western Hotel.

Gondoliers, alias Bill Slade, Arthur Shephard and Eric Nicholson, 1925. This photograph was taken by Ernest Berry.

The Operatic Society in costume for their 1925 production of Gilbert and Sullivan's *The Gondoliers.*

Cole's Fair at Gillingham, before the First World War.

Outing to Gough's Caves at Cheddar in Mr Lawley's charabanc, 1920s. Polly and Nellie Dunning are the two passengers at the rear and a young Phil Read is next to the driver's seat.

May Day celebrations in Dr Walker's garden, Newbury, 1941. From left to right, back row: Brenda White, Pam Wadham, Joyce Hooper, Betty Coombs, Sheila Coombs, Janet Stocker, Daphne Bland, Esther Harding, Hazel White, Colleen Raymond, Enid Gray, Pauline ?, Eileen Cross, -?-, Diana Case, Ruth Martin, Joan Luffman. Front row: Freda White, Pam Hillier, Molly Harding.

Blackmore Vale Hunt meeting in The Square.

Gillingham Imperial Silver Band with bandmaster Walt Morgan, 1936.

Tommy Trinder of radio, films and music hall fame takes the baton to the town's band during a special festival week, 20 June 1970. Robert Smith is the player who needs to pay attention!

Children's carnival, 1930.

King George V's Jubilee carnival, 1935. Phil Read holds 'The Gillingham Ox' sign.

Mr Arthur Bell (1891-1976), known affectionately as 'Dinger'. He was a founder member of the carnival when it was revived in the 1950s and loved to lead the procession, on this occasion in the 1960s, mounted on a donkey. After leaving Wyke School, he worked for Frank Burton as a butcher's boy and, following First World War service, he worked for GB Matthews at the brewery until his retirement in 1956. He was a very public-spirited citizen and was also involved with the British Legion, Silver Band and the football club.

'Spivs' Robert Budd and Terry Lush operate in Station Road on Carnival Day, *c.* 1955.

Ted Willis celebrates his ninetieth birthday at the Haig Club (now the Royal British Legion), c. 1960. From left to right, back row: Mick O'Dea, Bill Slade, Sid Carter, Archie Rose. Front row: Mr Gould, Ted Jones, Kim Comben, Ted Willis.

The Buffalo darts team, 1940s. The team includes: Joe Dolman, Archie Doggrell, Mark Fry, Reg Cross, Cyril Sims and ? White.

The Fir Tree pub's outing to Weston-Super-Mare, 1946. The Fir Tree was situated on the Mere Road and is now a private residence.

Coronation Club presentation night supper, 1950s.

Gillingham Jazz Band, 1927. The band raised funds to restart the old Town Band, which has been going strong ever since.

Phil Wiseman & The Travellers, 1958. From left to right: Dave Bennett, Tony Martin, Sam Pike, Phil Wiseman, Ken Newport, Dave Wathen and Mervyn Miles.

Swimming bath in Hardings Lane, 1960. This was opened in June 1959 and dedicated to 'Those Who Served 1939-1945'. Funds raised by the Welcome Home Committee were invested and eventually used for this worthwhile project. The baths are now covered and part of the Leisure Centre.

Hockey team, 1955. From left to right, back row: Theresa Suter, Joyce Foster, Marion Blanchard, Sally Pike, Hazel Flower, Vera Collis. Front row: Molly Griffiths, Yvonne Birchall, Janet Smart, Beryl Knapton, Helen Burt. Bill Foster is the umpire.

Preparations in Station Road for the visit of the as-yet-uncrowned Queen Elizabeth and Prince Philip, 1952. After leaving the station, the princess would proceed to Mere via Station Road, High Street, Queen Street, Bay Road and Lawn Cross Road. Over the next ten years, she made several unofficial visits to the National Stud at Sandley. The next official visit was not until 1990, on her way to see her grandchildren at Port Regis School.

Visit of Her Majesty the Queen on 3 July 1952. The Queen arrived at Gillingham station at 2.15pm. The Earl of Shaftesbury, Lord Lieutenant of the County, presented Mr E. Batho (chairman of the parish council) and Mr F.W. Davis (clerk to the parish council). Large numbers of local school children greeted the Queen outside the station entrance. Elizabeth King, who was accompanied by Isobel Case, presented a bouquet of flowers from the schools. In the background is Mrs Brocklebank, who presented a specially bound copy of *The Marn'll Book*.

Local dignitaries raise a glass to toast Sherman's new building in Station Road. Mr George Hoy, founder and chairman, laid a commemorative stone on 7 May 1975.

Shermans' Christmas Dinner, *c.* 1964. From left to right, back row (standing): Trevor Howard, Ken Tottle, Geoff Hacker, Bob Biss, Tom ?, Richard Gould. Back row (seated): Mr and Mrs Webster, Herbert Hoy, Mrs Hoy, George and Mrs Hoy, Mr and Mrs Howard. Other diners: -?-, George Davis, Robert Simpson, John Ayres, Mrs Case Mr Case, Barry Whittaker, Ron Kemp, Tony Ritchen, Pam Collis, Mr and Mrs Wiles, Ray Gulliford. Ann Tregurtha, Chris Marsh, Mrs Marsh, Kath Anker, Pete Towndrow, -?-, Pam Dyke, Pat Pickford, Sid Pickford, Bert King.

Gillingham Brownies at the 1964 carnival, commemorating fifty years of their organisation. From left to right: Julia Johnson, Carol Dear, Sue Moore, Evelyn Stokes, Margret Welbourne, Alison Hardy, Rachel Suttle, Sandra Weeks, Jane Gurnett, Anita Scott, -?-, Rachel Green, Clare Luffman, Anne Newcombe, Penny Abbot and Angela Rice.

The Youth Club football team, 1974. Back row, from left to right: Colin Lucas, Robert Gray, Mark Farrand, Mike Loader, Ray Miles, Bob Biss, Robert Smith, Tommy Biss. Front row: Gerald Matthews, Dave Hardiman, Mike Lloyd, Dave Hoskins, Owen Pritchard, Stuart Hacker, John Hillier.

Rover Scouts and Senior Scouts belonging to St Mary's Troop with the group scoutmaster, Canon E.L. Seager, about to set off for a fortnight's holiday in Brittany, August 1955.

Floods in the High Street, July 1982.

Herbie, Alan and John Light of W.H. Light & Co., Newbury, 1950s. Formerly makers of the Magnet cycle and suppliers of motorcycles, it is today a Texaco garage.

The mill, showing flood and fire damage, 1982.

Wiles Bakery, Hardings Lane, 1948.

Clearing up the river and river bank, 1970s. The War Memorial was later removed to the car park and the buildings in the background were demolished in 1996.

Gillingham Town Council, 1977. From left to right, back row: -?-, E. Samways, M. Osmond, F. Shepherd (clerk), F. Evill, Mrs K. DeGruchy, T. Raisebeck, Mrs C. Raisebeck, R. Weeks, C. Howe, Mrs H. Burt. Front row: S. Hiscott, A. Coombs, S. Ballard (mayor), G. Jones.

Committee and helpers of the Local History Society on the day the new museum was officially opened by society president, Herbert Green, October 1996. From left to right: David Lloyd (vice-chairman), John Juddery, Alan Whiffen, Joan Jaggard, Mr Coates, Peter Crocker (chairman), Glynis Crocker, Nigel Gates (asst. curator), Mrs Dowle (librarian), Lyn Light (curator), Herbie Light, Ken Fisher, Library Asst, John Pinnock, Ralph Allman (secretary), Pearl Coates, Bob Walton and Dave Hiscock. Gillingham Museum became the first recipient of a Heritage Lottery Award.